LEVEL ONE
Sounding it out

Ripley® Readers

Learning to read. Reading to learn!

LEVEL ONE **Sounding It Out** Preschool–Kindergarten
For kids who know their alphabet and are starting to sound out words.

learning sight words • beginning reading • sounding out words

LEVEL TWO **Reading with Help** Preschool–Grade 1
For kids who know sight words and are learning to sound out new words.

expanding vocabulary • building confidence • sounding out bigger words

LEVEL THREE **Independent Reading** Grades 1–3
For kids who are beginning to read on their own.

introducing paragraphs • challenging vocabulary • reading for comprehension

LEVEL FOUR **Chapters** Grades 2–4
For confident readers who enjoy a mixture of images and story.

reading for learning • more complex content • feeding curiosity

Ripley Readers Designed to help kids build their reading skills and confidence at any level, this program offers a variety of fun, entertaining, and unbelievable topics to interest even the most reluctant readers. With stories and information that will spark their curiosity, each book will motivate them to start and keep reading.

PUBLISHING

Vice President, Licensing & Publishing Amanda Joiner
Editorial Manager Carrie Bolin

Editor Jessica Firpi
Writer Korynn Wible-Freels
Designer Mark Voss
Reprographics Bob Prohaska

Published by Ripley Publishing 2020

10 9 8 7 6 5 4 3 2 1

Copyright © 2020 Ripley Publishing

ISBN: 978-1-60991-341-0

No part of this publication may be reproduced in whole or in part, stored in a retrieval system, or transmitted in any form by any means, electronic, mechanical, photocopying, recording, or otherwise, without written permission from the publisher.

For more information regarding permission, contact:
VP Licensing & Publishing
Ripley Entertainment Inc.
7576 Kingspointe Parkway, Suite 188
Orlando, Florida 32819

Email: publishing@ripleys.com
www.ripleys.com/books
Manufactured in China in January 2020.

First Printing

Library of Congress Control Number: 2019954284

RIPLEY Readers

Baby Animals!

All true and unbelievable!

RIPLEY PUBLISHING

a Jim Pattison Company

Baby animals are so cute!

A baby dog
is a puppy.

They like to
run and play!

This white puppy will
get black spots one day!

A baby cat is
a kitten.

They sleep a lot.

Kittens have blue eyes.

A tiger mom
helps her cubs
find food.

You can see a yellow chick
at a farm.

If it comes
from an egg,
it does not have
a belly button.

A baby deer is a fawn.

It has white spots.

Baby hippos are big!

Hippos cannot swim. Wow!

A baby panda
is not born
black and white.

It is pink!

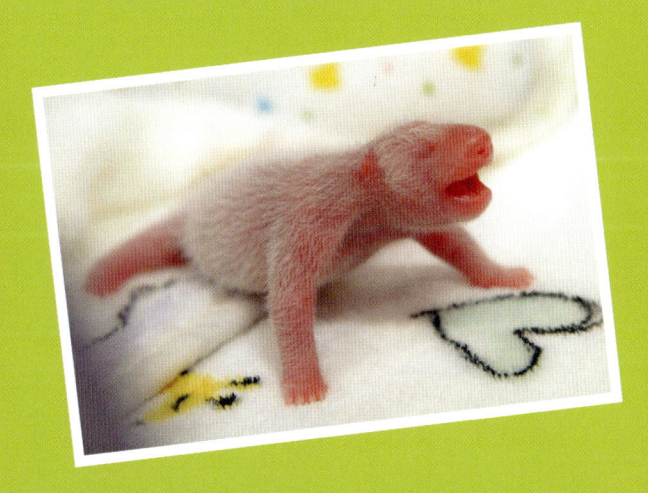

Baby fish are too small to see!

Look!

This bunny
wants to say hi!

Bye!

Ready for More?

Ripley Readers feature unbelievable but true facts and stories!

For more information about Ripley's Believe It or Not!, go to www.ripleys.com